I HATE
THIS PLACE

I HATE THIS PLACE

The Pessimist's Guide to Life

Jimmy Fallon and Gloria Fallon

TV Books
New York

Library of Congress Catologing-in-Publication Data
Fallon, Jimmy and Gloria.
    I hate this place : the pessimist's guide to life / by Jimmy Fallon and Gloria Fallon.
      p. cm.
    ISBN 1-57500-049-0 (pbk.)
    1. Conduct of life Humor. 2. Pessimism Humor. I. Fallon, Gloria. II. Title.
PN6231.C6142F35 1999
818'.5402—dc21   99-41386
                                                                        CIP

The publisher has made every effort to secure permission to reproduce copyrighted material and would like to apologize should there have been any errors or omissions.

TV Books, L.L.C.
1619 Broadway, Ninth Floor
New York, NY 10019
www.tvbooks.com

Design by Anthony Knight.
Illustrations by Robert Kopecky.
Manufactured in Canada

Contents

Dedication

This book is dedicated to our grandmother, Gloria Feeley,
who after reading the first manuscript said, "This book stinks."
We love and miss you.

Pessimist's Prologue

Are you tired of looking for the sunny side of the street? The pot of gold at the end of the rainbow? The silver lining in every cloud? I am. I've never found any of these things, have you?

Are you sick of reading those meditational self-help books that are supposed to win you friends, give you inner peace, and make you rich? I am—and why? They don't work, and that's that. I'm here to tell you the truth, plain and simple, in my complete guidebook compiled from my own experiences. This book will provide you with daily affirmations tailored to destroy any illusions you might have. It will warn you of situations that will surely lead to embarrassment. It will explain in simpler English what people are really trying to say when they talk to you, and it will relate some of my personal reflections and bitter experiences.

So, you can take my advice or leave it. Call me a pessimist, call me a grouch, it doesn't matter to me. Because guess what? We don't make that much of a difference to each other anyway.

Sincerely,

The Pessimist

Chapter One:

*If You Were
Thinking Of . . .*

Going to Happy Hour to meet some new friends:

Think again. You'll be the only person without a friend or a date,
and you're too shy to just go up and introduce yourself to strangers.
You're just going to sit by yourself, paying for drink after drink,
until you're a pathetic, quivering mass at the bottom of your barstool.
It'll turn out to be Sad Hour instead, for you and everyone involved.

Having a birthday party:

For what? To celebrate how many years you've been dragging yourself around on this earth? Anyway, only surprise birthday parties take away the stress and embarrassment of nobody showing up. At least then you can say, "Well, I didn't want a stupid party anyway."

Calling up an old friend after a long time:

Seriously rethink this. Any conversation that begins with

"Hey, remember me?" is doomed from the get-go.

Leaving the house:

This is okay, just remember that you will most likely run into
people you don't want to talk to, and also there is more
of a chance that you can get killed.

Going to a family reunion:

Your immediate family is bad enough. Do you really want to see the people who are responsible for starting this whole mess?

If You Were Thinking Of...

Buying a car:

Remember there is a possibility that
this could be your coffin.

Going dancing:

Sure, people have fun dancing, right?
Yeah, they'll have more fun watching you do
the "Can't Buy Me Love" dance by yourself.

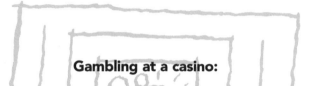

Gambling at a casino:

Do you think that after all these years you're going to be lucky?

You might as well throw your money out the window—

at least then you won't have to pay for a lonely hotel room.

Listening to music:

Well it's one for the money, two for the show,

three to get ready and…change this song,

it's giving me a goddamn headache!

If You Were Thinking Of...

Going to the wedding you were invited to:

Just send a card with money, that's all

they really wanted anyway.

Buying a new pair of expensive sneakers:

Don't you watch the news?
People are getting killed out there for new sneakers!

**Talking to that person you think
is "giving you the eye":**

Keep your mouth shut. The only reason they keep looking at you

is because you probably have some food stuck in your teeth.

Seeing a foreign movie:

Look at picture...look at words...look at picture...look at words...
look at me getting the hell out of the movie theater.

Exercising:

You'll probably just break your ankle or twist your knee.

You have to be in shape to get into shape—

it's a no-win situation, like so many others.

If You Were Thinking Of...

Going to the laundromat to meet people:

Just say you luck out and meet someone that's interested in you. Do you really want to be with a person who can't afford a washer and dryer?

Chapter Two:

When People Say . . .

When people say...

"Let me have your number."

They really mean:

"Let me have your number so that I don't have to give you mine."

When people say...

"Hey, we'll get together."

They really mean:

"I hope I never run into you again!"

When people say...

"Oh, look what time it is!"

They really mean:

"And while you're looking, I'm leaving!"

When people say...

"Thank you for your application. Your résumé

was extremely impressive."

They really mean:

"You didn't get the job, and I blew my nose in your résumé."

When people say...

"Hey, is that new?"

They really mean:

"I hope you kept the receipt."

When people say…

"Are we having fun or what?"

They really mean:

"What."

When people say...

"Hey there...uh...buddy!"

They really mean:

"I have no idea what your name is, nor do I even care."

When people say...

"You have that 'retro' look."

They really mean:

"You're really trying hard to look young."

When people say...

"What are you doing later?"

They really mean:

"I hope you aren't going to be where I am later."

When people say...

"Well, that's very interesting."

They really mean:

"What you just said is so boring that I don't even want to add a little information of my own to it. I'd rather just classify it as 'interesting' and not be associated with it at all."

When people say...

"Oh, can you hold on a minute? I have another call."

They really mean:

"Thank God for the mute button!
I'll just say it's my aunt calling long-distance."

When people say…

"I've got a train to catch, so I'd better get going."

They really mean:

"What a great way to end this infernal conversation!"

When people say...

"Hey, I didn't expect to see you here!"

They really mean:

"Who the hell invited this jerk?"

When people say...

"Don't worry about it—this round is on me."

They really mean:

"And the next four are going to be on you, dork."

When people say…

"You look different today."

They really mean:

"You look sick."

When people say...

"That's so sweet of you! You are so sweet!"

They really mean:

"Thanks, ass-kisser!"

When people say...

"I'm sorry—I forgot your name."

They really mean:

"I just want you to feel as unimportant as I think you are."

When people say . . .

"To each his own!"

They really mean:

"Weirdo!"

When people say...

"I hate to say 'I told you so,' but..."

They really mean:

"Nya, nya! Told you so!"

When people say...

"That's the way the cookie crumbles."

They really mean:

"Sucks to be you, pal."

When people say...

"I've never met anyone like you before."

They really mean:

"I never want to meet anyone like you again."

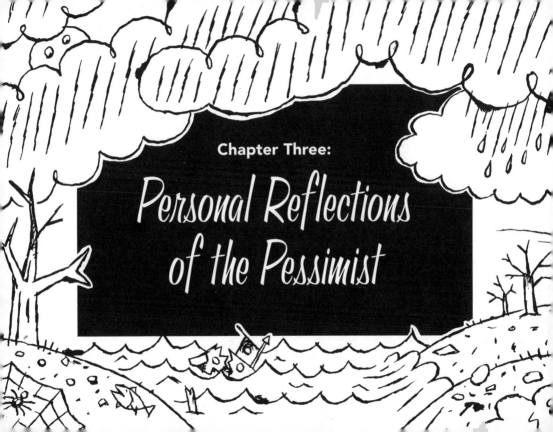

Chapter Three:

*Personal Reflections
of the Pessimist*

Some days, I wake up and stare at the ceiling.

Then I think, "Man, I wish it was tomorrow."

I'm starting to think that I'm the butt of
a joke that the whole world is in on.

Growing up, I always wanted to be just like Abe Lincoln.

Dead.

I usually avoid people who are nice to me, because
I know they're just going to ask for a favor sooner or later.

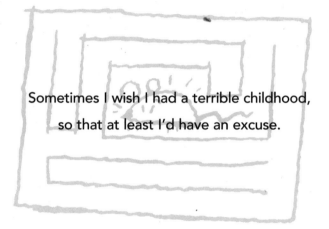

Sometimes I wish I had a terrible childhood,

so that at least I'd have an excuse.

There's nothing better than a day in the sun, if you can ignore all the ultraviolet rays that give you skin cancer.

Personal Reflections of the Pessimist

Everyone keeps telling me to travel and see the world
because that's where all of the opportunities are.
Like the opportunity that I'll get killed in a foreign country!

Personal Reflections of the Pessimist

Someone should invent action figures that are lanky and have no super powers. Then the youth of today might respect people like me.

Personal Reflections of the Pessimist

Sometimes I think, "This is all a test to see how strong you are.

There must be something higher after this, some reward..."

Then I think, "Yeah right, wake up and smell your instant coffee."

Sometimes I cross the street with my eyes shut.

If I'm ever at a party, I always take drinks from other people, hoping someone put something in it.

Personal Reflections of the Pessimist

Every time I talk to someone, I know I'm just wasting their time.

Personal Reflections of the Pessimist

I often try to reassure myself by saying,

"Well, at least it can't get any worse." But the truth is,

it always can. And that's what really terrifies me.

They say a dog is man's best friend.

That's if you're lucky enough to get one of those "friendly" dogs.

Sometimes I think the reason I don't get along

with anyone else is because I'm superior.

Then I think to myself, "What's so great about me?"

I have a hard time looking at myself, let alone other people.

People seem to enjoy saying, "Is this glass half-full or half-empty?" They stop smiling when I say, "It'll be empty when I pour it over your head."

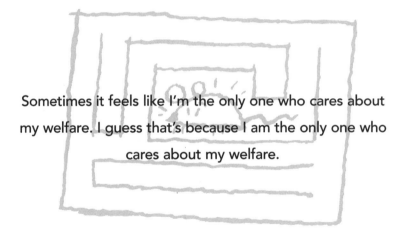

Sometimes it feels like I'm the only one who cares about my welfare. I guess that's because I am the only one who cares about my welfare.

When I see professional clowns, mimes, or people
that make balloon animals, I always think of their relatives
and how disappointed they must be.

People say that Nostradamus predicted both world wars,
the rise of Hitler, and the assassination of Kennedy.
Too bad he put it in a code that no one could understand
until the events happened. Some prophet he was.

Chapter Four:

My Story

My Story

I bought a package of low-fat cookies that had 50 percent more cookies in the box than usual, so if I ate the whole box I'd gain more weight than if it was a regular-size box of cookies. They should call these types of cookies "High-Fats" 'cause that's what everyone's going to say when I walk in the room.

My Story

I went to a fast food restaurant and had to wait twenty minutes.
I wasn't mad that I didn't get my food quickly. I was simply outraged
that someone else was in control of wasting my time.

My Story

Why should I date? Oh, I know! Just so I can get to know
a person so well that I start to get attached to them,
spend my money on them, neglect my friends and family,
and then get dumped so that I'm worse off than I ever was.

My Story

As if my social life wasn't bleak enough, Caller ID had to come along. My number might as well be listed as "Don't Pick Up the Phone."

My Story

When people talk to me, I usually nod my head and
agree with whatever they are saying. If they continue to talk,
I usually say, "Are you still talking to me, horseface?"

My Story

I don't use clocks to tell time. I use them more as a countdown to see how much time is left in another sad day of my life.

My Story

Did you ever sit back and evaluate your life and think,

"Boy, things are going just as I always wanted them to?"

I didn't think so.

My Story

My pet rock is the only one I trust in this world.

My Story

I never "live in the past" like some people who go to therapy—
the past was bad enough while it was happening.

My Story

When my parents told me that there was no Santa Claus,
I wasn't surprised. Once I had found out all the other kids got
presents from this "Santa," I put two and two together.

My Story

When people call my name, I automatically assume that they are talking to someone else.

My Story

I don't think I'll ever get married. I can barely accept myself "for better or worse, richer or poorer."

My Story

I think people who run in marathons are crazy.

I wouldn't do it even if I was guaranteed to win.

Sweating like a pig, accepting little cups of water from strangers,

and having diarrhea run down my legs in public for a cheap

medal just isn't worth it, as far as I'm concerned.

My Story

Everyone keeps telling me to put more of my hard-earned
money into my retirement fund. Why?
So when I'm sixty-five I can afford to have that new hip put in?

My Story

I remember when I was growing up I used to have one of those imaginary friends. The only problem was that he ignored me.

My Story

Most kids get excited when it snows, thinking of sleighriding and snowmen. I used to think of the increased amount of car accidents the snow would bring.

My Story

I don't go to "amusement" parks.

Call me crazy, but spinning around in circles and watching

kids throw up cotton candy just doesn't amuse me.

My Story

I hate public transportation, but here's an effective way
to deal with it: Pour coffee on the seat next to you.
Not only can no one sit there, but you get the joy of seeing
everyone's disappointment once they realize they can't sit down.

My Story

Whenever I'm stuck in traffic, I can't help but wonder,
"Where did the creator of 'The Jetsons' go, and why hasn't
he done something about this??"

Chapter Five:

Optimistic Advice You Should Never Follow

The Early Bird Catches the Worm

Exactly.

Live Each Day As If It Were Your Last

So you want me to lie around in a hospital bed
with an I.V. and an oxygen tank? My last day's going to be
bad enough without rehashing it day after day!

Optimistic Advice You Should Never Follow

Keep Your Chin Up

Why—so that everyone can look up your nose?

A Stitch in Time Saves Nine

Save all the time you want stitching.

Hiring a tailor not only saves you the nine stitches, but all the

time you'd waste trying to thread the needle.

Smoking Is Bad for Your Health

Who died and made these people Surgeon General?

As if the Apocalypse isn't around the corner anyway.

Wise up, people!

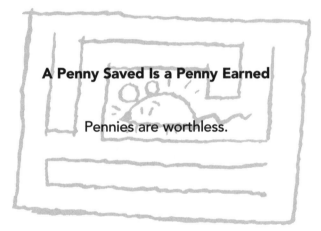

A Penny Saved Is a Penny Earned

Pennies are worthless.

Don't Put Off 'Til Tomorrow What You Can Do Today

And if you die in your sleep tonight, you wasted your
last day on Earth doing laundry.

Life Is What You Make It

So I'm the one to blame for all this?

There's Plenty of Fish in the Sea

And most are like the one who just dumped you.

Shape Up or Ship Out

Shut up.

Chapter Six:

Daily Affirmations for the Pessimist

Tomorrow may never come.

I am a rock, and a rock feels no pain.

Apathy is the highest virtue.

If you don't have anything nice to say, welcome to the club.

Don't try beating 'em or joining 'em.

Either hang out by yourself, or quit.

Today is another day, just like yesterday was.

Every cloud has a silver lining, and in that lining is probably the rain.

I have absolutely no control of my future.

If I keep my mouth shut, things will go a lot smoother.

Seek, and you shall be disappointed.

Knock, and the door shall be slammed in your face.

Everyone is out to get me.

Life is like a bowl.

Daily Affirmations for the Pessimist

Each man is an island.

Another day, another sixty-eight cents.

You win some, I lose some.

Life: live it, you don't have a choice anyway.

Wherever I go, there I am, and I hate this place.

A Final Note from the Pessimist

First of all, I would like to thank you for purchasing and reading this collection of life's ordinary occurrences as seen through my eyes (unless you stole this book or got it as a gift). If I made you look at the world in a different way, or made you laugh at my day-to-day realizations, then I did my job. I let you see the world of a pessimist, and, as you can probably tell, it's not much fun.

But a word of caution: if the revelations in this book made you feel a bit depressed, then you have read the book wrong. Go back to the start and read it again, remembering that I'm the pessimist, not you. If you are still depressed, then you might be a pessimist yourself, and I seriously suggest that you get some help and start reading those meditational "find your soul" type of books. I don't mind helping others, since we pessimists have to stick together. But if you ever see me on the street, please don't say "Hi" because I probably wouldn't want to hear anything you have to say anyway.

Until then, don't keep reaching for the stars, because you'll just look like an idiot, stretching like that for no reason.

Sincerely,
The Pessimist

About the Authors

Jimmy and Gloria Fallon were born a year apart in Brooklyn, New York, to Jim and Gloria Fallon (yes, you read that correctly), and were raised upstate in Saugerties. They both attended college in the Albany area. After college the two Fallons went their separate ways, moving to Los Angeles and Boston respectively. **I Hate This Place** started as cross-country e-mail messages between brother and sister, making each other laugh while they were miles apart. With Jimmy's background in comedy and Gloria's background in writing, the two siblings decided to write a book, which is what you are holding now. While they are excited about having their first book published, the Fallons still hate this place.